You Can't Build A Treehouse Without A Tree

Written By:

P.J. Belding

Illustrated By:

Amurtha Godage

For permissions and inquiries please contact the author: olpartridge@gmail.com

Illustrations by Amurtha Godage

Published in Canada
ISBN (Paperback Edition): 978-1-7387080-6-2
ISBN (E-book Edition):   978-1-7387080-7-9

Dedicated to my three seriously stubborn kids

Brady woke up one morning and decided he was going to build a treehouse.

"Where are you going with all those tools, Brady?" asked the father.

"I'm going to build a treehouse today," said Brady.

"A treehouse?" asked the mother. "What do you mean you're going to build treehouse?"

"Don't worry mom. I know what I'm doing."

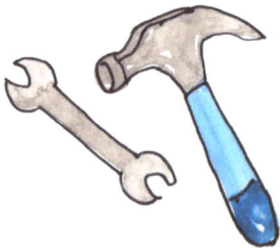

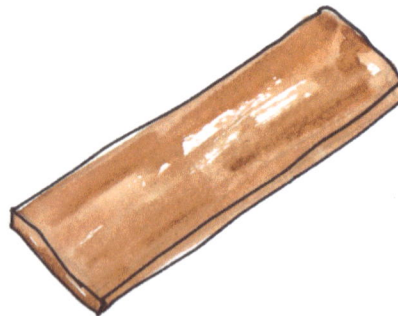

Brady opened the front door, stepped outside and looked to the right. No trees. He looked to the left. No trees. He looked all the way down the street…no trees. "Hmmmm…" he said. "I know! Backyard!"

Brady marched all the way through the house to the backyard. He looked to the right….no trees. He looked to the left…no trees. All he could see were houses. No trees. House after house after house. But still no trees.

He went back inside.

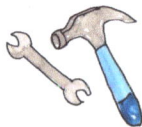

"Brady, what's wrong, I thought you were going to build a treehouse?" asked the father.

"I was going to build a treehouse," said Brady. "I have all the tools to build a treehouse. I have a saw, I have a hammer, I have nails, and I have some boards, but…I don't have a tree! How am I supposed to build a treehouse without a tree?"

"Well," said the father. "You can't build a treehouse without a tree."

The next day, the parents went downstairs for breakfast. Instead of a breakfast table in the kitchen, there was a treehouse on the table. "Brady! What have you done to the table?" asked the father.

"Well… you can't build a treehouse without a tree, so I built a treehouse on the table instead. Do you like it?"

"Brady, that's not a treehouse. It's a tablehouse. Besides, you can't build a house where people need to eat their food," said the father.

"Says who?" asked Brady.

"Says me!" said the father.

The next day the mother wanted to have a bath, but there was a treehouse in the bathtub. "Brady, what have you done to the bathtub?"

"You can't build a treehouse without a tree. And you can't build a treehouse on the table because it's where people eat their food. So, I built a treehouse in the bathtub instead. Do you like it?"

"Brady, it's not a treehouse, it's a bathtub house. And besides, you can't build a house where people need to wash. You'll have to take it all down."

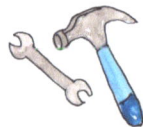

The next day, the parents went downstairs to the basement and found that Brady had built a treehouse on the treadmill. "Brady, what have you done to the treadmill?" asked the father.

"Well…you can't build a treehouse without a tree, and you can't build a treehouse where people eat their food, and you can't build a treehouse where people need to wash. So… I built a treehouse on the treadmill. Nobody ever uses a treadmill."

"Yes, but we *MIGHT* use the treadmill someday. You can't build a house on something people *MIGHT* use," said the father. "You'll have to take it all down and build your treehouse somewhere else."

So, Brady took his tool box and his tool belt, and he set out to find somewhere else to build his treehouse. He walked all the way into downtown Toronto.

He looked all around but people were using everything, the subway, the hotdog stand, the police station, the bank, the benches, and even the subway tunnel.

SUBWAY 2

Then Brady looked way up. He saw the perfect place to build his treehouse.

His parents came looking for him. It wasn't hard to find him because everyone in the city was looking way up.

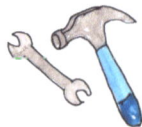

At the top of the CN Tower, Brady built a treehouse.

Brady's father grabbed the loudspeaker from the policeman and shouted, "Brady! What are you doing?"

Brady shouted back to his father, "I built a treehouse!"

"But that's not a treehouse…it's a…it's a…skyhouse!

Brady's mother grabbed the loudspeaker and shouted, "Brady you can't build a treehouse on a skyscraper. It's too windy up there. It's too cold, it's too high, it's too…"

Brady's father grabbed the loudspeaker from the mother and shouted, "Brady, it's time to come home for supper."

Since Brady had been
out all day looking for a
place to build his treehouse,
he was getting hungry and
a little tired. He came down
and went home.

The next day, the parents were waiting for Brady by the backdoor. They were holding watering cans.

"What are those for?" asked Brady.

"We prepared something for you. Go outside and see," said the mother.

"Baby trees!" shouted Brady.

He watered the trees every day.

And he was happy.

Many years later,
there was a forest in the neighborhood…

And a treehouse just for ol' Brady.

More books in the *Seriously Stubborn Kids* series

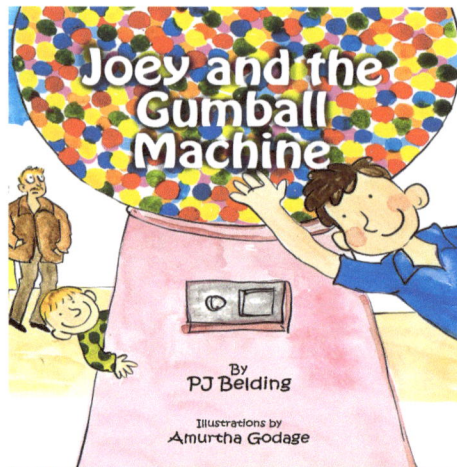

Joey and the Gumball Machine

By
PJ Belding

Illustrations by
Amurtha Godage

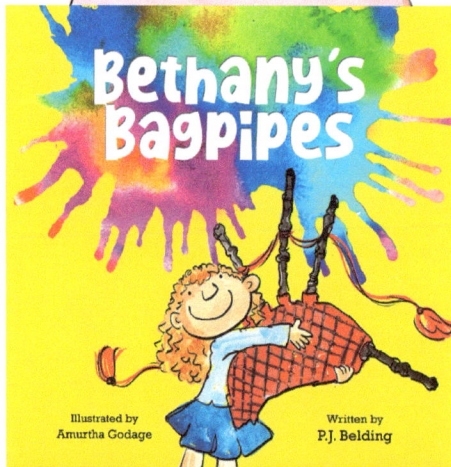

Bethany's Bagpipes

Illustrated by
Amurtha Godage

Written by
P.J. Belding

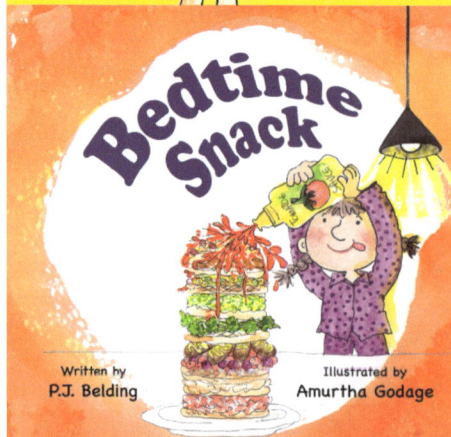

Bedtime Snack

Written by
P.J. Belding

Illustrated by
Amurtha Godage

www.ingramcontent.com/pod-product-compliance
Lightning Source LLC
LaVergne TN
LVHW072115070426
835510LV00002B/59